The Quotation Bank

An Inspector Calls

J.B Priestley

Copyright © 2022 Esse Publishing Limited

First published in 2016 by:
The Quotation Bank ®
Esse Publishing Limited

10 9 8

A CIP catalogue record for this book is available from the British Library.
ISBN 978-0-9956086-2-7

All enquiries to: contact@thequotationbank.co.uk

Printed and bound by Target Print Limited, Broad Lane, Cottenham, Cambridge CB24 8SW.

www.thequotationbank.co.uk

Introduction

Quotations

Revision and Essay Planning

Welcome to The Quotation Bank, the comprehensive guide to all the key quotations you need to succeed in your exams.

Whilst you may have read the play, watched a production, understood the plot and have a strong grasp of context, the vast majority of marks awarded in your GCSE are for the ability to write a focused essay, full of quotations, and most importantly, quotations that you then analyse.

I think we all agree it is analysis that is the tricky part – and that is why we are here to help!

The Quotation Bank takes 25 of the most important quotations from the text, interprets them, analyses them, highlights literary techniques Priestley has used, puts them in context, and suggests which quotations you might use in which essays.

At the end of **The Quotation Bank** we have put together a sample answer, essay plans and great revision exercises to help you prepare for your exam. We have also included a detailed glossary to make sure you completely understand what certain literary terms actually mean!

English Literature 9-1: What are examiners looking for?

All GCSE Exam Boards mark your exams using the same Assessment Objectives (AOs) – around 80% of your mark across the English Literature GCSE will be awarded for A01 and A02.

A01	Read, understand and respond to texts. Students should be able to: • Maintain a critical style and develop an *informed personal response* • Use textual references, *including quotations*, to support and illustrate *interpretations*.
A02	Analyse the *Language, Form and Structure* used by a writer to *create meanings and effects*, using *relevant subject terminology* where appropriate.

Basically, **AO1** is the ability to answer the question set, showing a good knowledge of the text, and using quotations to back up ideas and interpretations.

AO2 is the ability to analyse these quotations, as well as the literary techniques the writer uses, and to show you understand the effect of these on the audience.

We will also highlight elements of **AO3** – the context in which the play is set.

How The Quotation Bank can help you in your exams.

The Quotation Bank is designed to make sure that every point you make in an essay clearly fulfils the Assessment Objectives an examiner will be using when marking your work.

Every quotation comes with the following detailed material:

Interpretation: The interpretation of each quotation allows you to fulfil **AO1**, responding to the text and giving an informed personal response.

Techniques: Using subject-specific terminology correctly (in this case, the literary devices used by Priestley) is a key part of **AO2**.

Analysis: We have provided as much analysis (**AO2**) as possible. It is a great idea to analyse the quotation in detail – you need to do more than just say what it means, but also what effect the language, form and structure has on the audience.

Use in essays on…Your answer needs to be focused to fulfil **AO1**. This section helps you choose relevant quotations and link them together for a stronger essay.

How to use The Quotation Bank.

Many students spend time learning quotations by heart.

This is an excellent idea, but they often forget what they are meant to do with those quotations once they get into the exam!

By using **The Quotation Bank**, not only will you have a huge number of quotations to use in your essays, you will also have ideas on what to say about them, how to analyse them, how to link them together, and what questions to use them for.

For GCSE essay questions, these quotations can form the basis of your answer, making sure every point comes directly from the text **(AO1)** and allowing you to analyse language, form and structure **(AO2)**. We also highlight where you can easily and effectively include context **(AO3)**.

For GCSE questions that give you an extract to analyse, the quotations in **The Quotation Bank** are excellent not only for revising the skills of analysis **(AO2)**, but also for showing wider understanding of the text **(AO1)**.

Act One:
 STAGE DIRECTIONS: "The lighting should be pink and intimate until the
     Inspector arrives, and then it should be brighter and harder."

Interpretation: The Birlings enjoy a lifestyle conducted away from the prying eyes
of society. When the Inspector arrives, his aim is to shine a light on their behaviour.

Techniques: Stage directions; Symbolism; Language.

Analysis:

- The lighting is symbolic of how the Birlings live their lives, and what the
  Inspector's role is in the play.
- "Pink" suggests both a luxurious lifestyle and a gentle, comfortable way of
  living. The Inspector brings a "brighter" light that foreshadows the fact that
  he intends to shine a light on the way they behave.
- "Intimate" has associations with a close knit family (or the closed ranks of
  the upper classes). The Inspector plans to expose this with a "harder" light.

Use in essays on…Class; Wealth; Authority.

Act One:
　　BIRLING: "I'm talking as a hard-headed, practical man of business."

Interpretation: Birling behaves as the patriarch (male head of the family) should do – society would expect him to be a provider for his family, unemotional and rational, focussing on the family business and maintaining their wealth.

Techniques: Alliteration; Language.

Analysis:
- The alliteration of the "h" sound in "hard-headed", a phrase Birling repeats frequently, has a cold tone, mimicking his coldness towards his workers.
- "Hard" shows Birling has no caring, compassionate side, and "headed" suggests he views things with his head, not heart – he has no sympathy.
- Birling is giving this speech at his daughter's engagement, yet he does not identify himself as a father or husband, but as a "practical man of business". His main role in society is as a businessman, not a father.

Use in essays on…Family; Marriage; Society.

Act One:
BIRLING: "Lady Croft – while she doesn't object to my girl – feels you might have done better for yourself socially."

Interpretation: Birling makes clear he knows that Lady Croft feels the Birlings are beneath them socially – to their generation, marriage is about social status, not love.

Techniques: Sentence structure; Language.

Analysis:

- Birling refers to Sheila as "my girl". It may be that this is said with a sense of pride, but the tone seems to be one of ownership rather than love.
- The phrase "done better" makes marriage seem like a competition Gerald has failed. The word "socially" has nothing to do with love or compassion, but entirely to do with public appearance.
- The hesitant sentence structure from Birling highlights how the upper classes don't talk openly and honestly – they prefer to keep things private.

Use in essays on…Family; Marriage; Society; Class; Love.

Act One:

  BIRLING: "I was Lord Mayor here two years ago when Royalty visited us. And I've always been regarded as a sound, useful party man. So – well – I gather there's a very good chance of a knighthood."

Interpretation: Birling is determined to show his value to Gerald and Lady Croft by emphasising his movement through the establishment and up the social ranks.

Techniques: Pronouns; Language; Semantic field.

Analysis:

- Birling doesn't focus on Sheila's value as a person – instead, he lists words from the semantic field of power and politics. "Lord Mayor", "Royalty" and "knighthood" focus on upper class hierarchy (social ranking) and influence.
- Being a "sound, useful party man" suggests Birling believes in hierarchy and not questioning those above you – when the "party" tell him to do or think something, he does it.

Use in essays on…Politics; Power; Society; Class.

Act One:

BIRLING: "Everybody has to look after everybody else, as if we were all mixed up together like bees in a hive – community and all that nonsense."

Interpretation: Birling dismisses the idea of community. The play is set pre-war but performed after World War Two, a time when the country had to come together.

Techniques: Simile; Tone.

Analysis:

- The simile refers to "bees", insects that are all workers, except a single queen bee – there would be no hierarchy for Birling to abuse. "A hive" is an enclosed space with nowhere to hide from responsibilities.
- Words such as "everybody", "together" and community" are dismissed by Birling as they suggest people need to take responsibility for others.
- Being "mixed up" would alter the class system that protects the Birlings, hence his dismissive and patronising tone when describing it as "nonsense".

Use in essays on…Responsibility; Power; Society; Class.

Act One:
 INSPECTOR: "She'd swallowed a lot of strong disinfectant. Burnt her inside out, of course."

Interpretation: The Inspector is determined to let the Birlings and the audience know just how horrific Eva Smith's death was, and the suffering she went through.

Techniques: Adverbs; Imagery; Adjectives; Tone.

Analysis:
- The Inspector makes Eva's suffering explicit. The adverb "a lot" highlights the desperate desire of Eva to die, and the adjective "strong" re-emphasises her determination to kill herself.
- The imagery of "burnt her inside out" emphasises her physical pain but also refers to how the Birlings similarly "burnt" her both inside and out.
- The Inspector's tone when he says "of course" may seem casual, but he shows the Birlings how their behaviour would "of course" lead to her death.

Use in essays on…Power; Society; Responsibility.

Act One:
> SHEILA: "But these girls aren't cheap labour – they're *people*."

Interpretation: For the first time, a Birling is beginning to show an understanding or empathy for the working classes and recognises they have rights too.

Techniques: Nouns; Imagery.

Analysis:
- The image of "these girls" as "cheap labour" makes them seem like machines, simply a tool for the upper classes to use. The plural "girls" shows they have no individual identity. For the first time, Sheila says they "aren't" just that – she recognises they have value as individuals, and younger characters are beginning to see that all people deserve to be treated fairly.
- The noun "people" has associations with community and responsibility to one another. It is the exact opposite of what Birling was saying earlier in the play and shows a growing generation gap between parents and children.

Use in essays on…Age; Society; Class.

Act One:
 INSPECTOR: "A nice little promising life there, I thought, and a nasty mess somebody's made of it."

Interpretation: Yet again, the Inspector deliberately understates the situation so that the audience dwell on just how horrifically the Birlings have behaved.

Techniques: Juxtaposition; Adjectives; Pronouns.

Analysis:

- The adjectives "nice little promising" all have positive associations, but also a tone of vulnerability. The use of the word "A" suggests Eva is not the only young woman destroyed by people like the Birlings.
- There is a clear juxtaposition between the "nice" and "promising" elements Eva brings to the world, and the "nasty mess" that the Birlings cause.
- The Inspector uses the pronoun "somebody" to emphasise the upper class hiding behind their status – no one will take responsibility for their actions.

Use in essays on…Power; Society; Class.

Act One:
  SHEILA: "How could I know what would happen afterwards? If she'd been
    some miserable plain little creature, I don't suppose I'd have done it."

Interpretation: Sheila is desperate to rid herself of guilt, and almost blames Eva for
being too pretty, as if that justifies her behaviour. It is a highly immature reaction.

Techniques: Adjectives; Questioning; Language.

Analysis:
  - The noun "creature" has animalistic associations – until now, Sheila saw
    those beneath her, such as Eva, as nothing more than animals.
  - The tone of her question shows a desperate need to excuse her behaviour.
    Unlike her parents, she begins to realise her behaviour has consequences.
  - The adjectives "miserable plain little" all emphasise the characteristics Sheila
    and the Birlings assume the working classes have – they have no right being
    "pretty" but instead should remain vulnerable and easy to manipulate.

Use in essays on…Prejudice; Age; Power.

Act Two:
  INSPECTOR: "And you think young women ought to be protected against
              unpleasant and disturbing things?"

Interpretation: The Inspector highlights the hypocrisy of Gerald when he tries to
protect Sheila as she is a "young woman", yet he didn't do the same for Eva.

Techniques: Irony; Adjectives; Rhetorical questions.

Analysis:
- The correct way for men to behave is to protect all "women" – the
  Inspector highlights the irony that the desire to protect Sheila was not how
  they treated Eva, emphasising their hypocrisy and double standards.
- The adjective "young" emphasises Eva's vulnerability. The Inspector's
  question shows the upper class being treated differently to the working class.
- The adjectives "unpleasant and disturbing" are again deliberately
  underwhelming – the treatment of Eva was far worse than this.

Use in essays on…Gender; Responsibility; Authority.

Act Two:
 INSPECTOR: "A girl died tonight. A pretty, lively sort of girl, who never did anybody any harm. But she died in misery and agony – hating life."

Interpretation: The Inspector explicitly shows the unjust nature of Eva's death.

Techniques: Sentence structure; Juxtaposition; Adjectives.

Analysis:
- The Birlings refer to that "sort of girl" throughout the play. The Inspector uses the adjectives "pretty, lively", which have positive associations, to contrast their prejudice, who use "sort of girl" as an insult.
- By referring to Eva as "she", the Inspector emphasises her lack of identity, and the words "misery and agony" confirm how little people cared for her.
- The short sentence "A girl died tonight" is emphatic and clear – there is no getting away from the brutal facts of the case. The innocence and youthfulness of "girl" is juxtaposed with the horror of "died".

Use in essays on…Age; Gender; Society.

Act Two:
 SHEILA: "I'm to blame – and I'm desperately sorry – but I can't believe – I won't believe – it's simply my fault that in the end she – committed suicide."

Interpretation: Whilst we have no sympathy for Sheila, we do see her accept blame and the beginning of a generational split between parents and children.

Techniques: Pronouns; Sentence structure; Repetition.

Analysis:
  • Sheila repeats the pronouns "I" and "my", focussing almost entirely on herself – she is still selfishly seeing the situation from her point of view.
  • Rather than controlled speech, her sentence structure is broken and stuttering, showing her true feelings, contrasting greatly with the somewhat staged speeches during the engagement party.
  • The use of "blame" and "fault" alongside "sorry" show the Inspector beginning to change the attitudes of the younger characters in the play.

Use in essays on…Age; Responsibility; Family.

Act Two:
 MRS BIRLING: "I don't suppose for a moment that we can understand why
                    the girl committed suicide. Girls of that class –"

Interpretation: Contrasting with Sheila's acceptance of her part in Eva's death, Mrs Birling repeatedly refuses to acknowledge any responsibility for Eva's suicide.

Techniques: Pronouns; Tone; Irony.

Analysis:
- Mrs Birling's prejudiced view of lower classes is clear. Sheila states they are "people" and the Inspector calls Eva "pretty, lively" – Mrs Birling refers to "that class" with a highly dismissive tone, suggesting they are all the same.
- "We" doesn't mean society as a whole, simply the upper class. "Understand" suggests the lower classes are completely alien to Mrs Birling.
- Mrs Birling is unwilling to think of Eva "for a moment" and is dismissive of "that class", ironic as she is part of a charity that helps "girls of that class".

Use in essays on…Responsibility; Class; Prejudice.

Act Two:

 GERALD: "Old Joe Meggarty, half-drunk and goggle-eyed, had wedged her into a corner with that obscene fat carcass of his."

Interpretation: Alderman Meggarty is presumed to be respectable due to his title. Gerald depicts the true nature of many of these supposedly respectable characters.

Techniques: Imagery; Names; Adjectives.

Analysis:

- The upper class hide behind titles such as "Lord Mayor", "Alderman" and "Lady". By referring to Meggarty as "Old Joe", his sophistication and power is removed and he becomes nothing more than a drunk old man.
- His "obscene fat carcass" gives Meggarty animalistic characteristics and "wedged her" suggests Eva was cornered like prey, unable to escape.
- The adjectives "half-drunk", "goggle-eyed" and "obscene" depict socially unacceptable behaviour. Gerald suggests this is a regular occurrence.

Use in essays on…Power; Politics; Gender.

Act Two:
 GERALD: "I suppose it was inevitable. She was young and pretty and warm-hearted – and intensely grateful."

Interpretation: Gerald is the only character who "had some affection for her". Gerald describes her character, increasing the injustice the audience feel at her death.

Techniques: Polysyndeton; Tri-colon (or list of three); Sentence structure.

Analysis:
- Eva's suicide is all the more unjust as she is depicted as such a wholesome character. The polysyndeton (repetition of 'and') in "young and pretty and warm-hearted – and intensely grateful" makes her qualities seem endless.
- The tri-colon emphasises she had a future ("young"), was attractive ("pretty"), but the sentence structure stresses "warm-hearted". It stands her out from Sheila, who is young and pretty, but certainly isn't warm-hearted.
- "Inevitable" assumes that if the upper class wants something, they get it.

Use in essays on…Marriage; Love; Gender.

Act Two:
    INSPECTOR: "Public men, Mr Birling, have responsibilities as well as privileges."

Interpretation: The core message of the play is that all people have responsibilities to one another. This is particularly important to the post-war audience.

Techniques: Statement; Collective nouns; Juxtaposition.

Analysis:

- This statement is directly addressed to Mr Birling but "Public men" emphasises the message of the play - all men have responsibilities.
- This statement is delivered as fact – Birling cannot argue with it. His weak reply of "Possibly" shows that Birling knows the Inspector is correct.
- The juxtaposition of "responsibilities" and "privileges" emphasises the difference between Birling and the Inspector. The Inspector sees the two as being entirely linked – Birling sees them as completely separate ideas.

Use in essays on…Responsibility; Class; Society; Politics; Power.

Act Two:
 INSPECTOR: "She was here alone, friendless, almost penniless, desperate.
  She needed not only money but advice, sympathy, friendliness."

Interpretation: The Inspector creates a very human image of Eva – she was not a
worker or a charitable case, but a human being who required support from others.

Techniques: Tri-colon; Juxtaposition; Abstract nouns.

Analysis:
- The image of a girl "alone" suggests vulnerability and isolation. The tri-
  colon refers to her struggling socially ("friendless"), economically
  ("penniless") and psychologically ("desperate").
- Her difficulties are juxtaposed with the solutions – "advice, sympathy,
  friendliness" are abstract nouns that cost nothing, yet Mrs Birling refused.
- "Needed" is a highly emotive word – Eva did not want or hope for support,
  she had an essential need for it to survive.

Use in essays on…Responsibility; Prejudice; Wealth; Society.

Act Three:
> ERIC: "Well, I was in that state when a chap easily turns nasty – and I threatened to make a row."

Interpretation: Eric explains events, whilst excusing the way he behaved – it seems that, contextually, being a man and being drunk justifies terrible behaviour.

Techniques: Juxtaposition; Euphemism.

Analysis:
- Eric's description as a "chap" has carefree, relaxed and friendly associations, juxtaposed with violent connotations of "nasty", "threatened" and "row".
- Eric's use of the noun "row" hints at a verbal argument, when it is clear Eric means he threatened physical violence, and "nasty" links to playground bullying, when he is alluding to physical and sexual abuse.
- The use of "when" and "easily" suggests that if an upper class man is "in that state", violence and abuse is inevitable, almost excusable.

Use in essays on…Power; Gender; Responsibility.

Act Three:

ERIC: "You killed her. She came to you to protect me – and you turned her away – yes, and you killed her – and the child she'd have had too – my child – your own grandchild – you killed them both – damn you, damn you."

Interpretation: A vile consequence of Eva's suicide is the death of her unborn child. Eric explicitly describes what they did to Eva and is overwhelmed with emotion.

Techniques: Sentence structure; Repetition; Language.

Analysis:

- The repetition of "child" conveys the death of innocence. Eric highlights that by killing Eva, they killed their own family – their "grandchild".
- The same is true for the repetition of the verb "killed" – the Birlings did not simply fire Eva, or refuse to help her, they ended her life.
- Eric should speak to his parents with respect. The stuttering sentences show Eric struggling with the consequences of his family's actions.

Use in essays on…Family; Age; Responsibility.

Act Three:
  INSPECTOR: "Just used her for the end of a stupid drunken evening, as if she was an animal, a thing, not a person. No, you won't forget."

Interpretation: The Inspector is coming to the end of his interrogation and reminds the Birlings, and the audience, just how degrading their treatment of Eva Smith was.

Techniques: Adjectives; Tri-colon.

Analysis:

- The Inspector's vocabulary is full of words that express just how senseless the Birling's treatment of Eva was – "just used", "end", "stupid drunken" and "evening" all highlight how fleeting and insignificant Eric saw the evening, contrasting greatly with the long term consequences of his actions.
- The tri-colon starts with two nouns that totally de-humanise Eva. "Animal" and "thing" suggest Eric doesn't even see her as "a person", but rather something he can simply use and control.

Use in essays on…Power; Society; Class.

Act Three:

INSPECTOR: "There are millions and millions and millions of Eva Smiths and John Smiths still left with us, with their lives, their hopes and fears, their suffering and chance of happiness."

Interpretation: The Inspector's final speech conveys Priestley's message to the audience. The Inspector claims Eva's story is not simply a one-off event.

Techniques: Polysyndeton; Listing; Contrasts.

Analysis:

- The polysyndeton emphasises the sheer scale of the issue facing society – the use of "and" makes the number of people just like Eva go on and on.
- The male "John Smiths" remind us this isn't about gender. Many of Eva's troubles were because she was female, but we have a duty to all people.
- Events in life contain negative "suffering", but only a "<u>chance</u> of happiness". Suffering is guaranteed, happiness is not.

Use in essays on…Gender; Prejudice; Class; Society.

Act Three:
  INSPECTOR: "What we think and say and do. We don't live alone. We are
     members of one body. We are responsible for each other."

Interpretation: Priestley's message is clear – we are all part of one world.

Techniques: Pronouns; Tri-colon; Sentence structure.

Analysis:
- The Birlings frequently refer to I, my, or them. The Inspector uses the pronouns "we" and "our" – we are a collective society, not individuals.
- The first tri-colon alludes to three ways we must change our behaviour if we are to survive as a society – actions ("do"), speech ("say") but also our values and beliefs ("think").
- The Inspector's sentence structure makes each of his statements sound like facts, and the repetition of "we are" leaves no room for the Birlings to argue against him.

Use in essays on…Responsibility; Society.

Act Three:

 INSPECTOR: "I tell you that the time will soon come when, if men will not learn that lesson, then they will be taught it in fire and blood and anguish."

Interpretation: The Inspector mimics Birling from Act One, using the same phrase Birling did – "I tell you". Whilst Birling looks foolish and arrogant as he is clearly wrong, the Inspector is wise and correctly foresees the future – the World Wars.

Techniques: Polysyndeton; Tri-colon; Dramatic irony; Imagery.

Analysis:
- The polysyndeton in "fire and blood and anguish" lengthens the scale of suffering we will endure, linking to the suffering of the World Wars.
- The tri-colon suggests suffering will destroy our landscape ("fire"), kill our communities ("blood") and cause immense emotional pain ("anguish").
- The dramatic irony is evident to the audience. Birling's predictions are incorrect, but the Inspector's chilling prediction is painfully accurate.

Use in essays on…Responsibility; Society.

Act Three:

ERIC: "You're beginning to pretend now that nothing's really happened at all. And I can't see it like that. This girl's still dead, isn't she?"

Interpretation: For Mr and Mrs Birling, if they are not going to get caught, then they believe their behaviour was acceptable, whereas Eric can't see it that way.

Techniques: Pronouns; Questions; Language.

Analysis:

- The divide between parents and children is shown in the use of pronouns, with Eric using "you're" compared with "I".
- The verb "pretend" refers to how the entire upper class behaves – they act in a certain way, and then "pretend" it was acceptable behaviour.
- The audience feel anger at the speed Mr and Mrs Birling revert to their old behaviour. The Inspector has been off stage for a few minutes, and although Eva is "still dead" they already see it as "nothing really happened".

Use in essays on…Responsibility; Age; Family; Society.

Act Three:
  BIRLING: "Now look at the pair of them – the famous younger generation
         who know it all. And they can't even take a joke."

Interpretation: Birling dismisses his children and their new view of the world in a
sarcastic manner to try to reassert his authority after the Inspector's departure.

Techniques: Tone; Language; Irony.

Analysis:

- Birling's patronising claim that they "know it all" is ironic. Everything he
  predicts is wrong – the Inspector and younger generation are indeed correct.
- Birling's tone is patronising. "The pair of them" makes Eric and Sheila seem
  like little children, and "famous younger generation" is aggressively sarcastic
  from a father determined to regain authority.
- The noun "joke" infuriates the audience – the idea that their behaviour can
  be passed off as a "joke" is disturbing and shows he has learnt nothing.

Use in essays on…Age; Prejudice; Family; Society.

Major Themes

Responsibility	Gender	Age
Prejudice	Class	Wealth
Marriage	Love	Power
Politics	Society	Family

Major Characters

Mr Birling	Mrs Birling	Sheila
Eric	Eva Smith	Gerald Croft
	The Inspector	

How to revise effectively.

One mistake people often make is to try to revise EVERYTHING!

This is clearly not possible.

Instead, once you know and understand the plot, a great idea is to pick three or four major themes, and three or four major characters, and revise these in great detail.

If, for example, you revised Mr Birling and Eva Smith, you will also have covered a huge amount of material to use in questions about Gender, Power or Class.

Or, if you revised Responsibility and Prejudice, you would certainly have plenty of material if a question on Sheila, Mrs Birling or Society was set.

Use the following framework as a basis for setting **any** of your own revision questions – simply swap the theme or character to create a new essay title!

How does Priestley portray the theme of _____ in *An Inspector Calls*?

How does the character of _____ develop as the play progresses?

How does Priestley explore the idea of abuse of power in An Inspector Calls?

Whilst power clearly belongs to the upper class in the play, it is frequently abused so as to hide their behaviour. When Gerald explains his part in Eva's death, the audience are exposed to the behaviour of "Alderman Meggarty". Just as Birling tried to exert power over the Inspector with the title of Lord Mayor, Alderman Meggarty is presumed to be respectable due to his title. Frequently, characters hide behind powerful titles such as "Lord Mayor", "Alderman" and "Lady" - when Gerald refers to Meggarty as "Old Joe", his sophistication and power is gone and he becomes nothing more than a drunk old man. Furthermore, the image of his "obscene fat carcass" gives Meggarty animalistic characteristics, and the image of having "wedged her" suggests Eva was being hunted, cornered like prey unable to escape – Meggarty is abusing his power to get what he wants. The adjectives "half-drunk", "goggle-eyed" and "obscene" depict a man behaving in a socially unacceptable manner; Gerald uses these terms as if this is a regular occurrence, and yet Mrs Birling only sees his powerful title, replying "surely you don't mean Alderman Meggarty?"

Potential Essay Questions

How does Priestley explore responsibility in the play?

Topic Sentence 1: Priestley explores the idea that responsibility is non-existent within the upper class.

Use: Pages 11, 19 and 29.

Topic Sentence 2: It seems Sheila believes she shouldn't be held accountable for her actions.

Use: Pages 15 and 18.

Topic Sentence 3: When we are responsible for others, it is usually within a family setting.

Use: Pages 16 and 25.

Topic Sentence 4: The message of the play is clear – we all have responsibilities.

Use: Pages 22 and 28.

How is gender explored in *An Inspector Calls*?

Topic Sentence 1: The play begins with depictions of women as a tool for marriage and for men to control.

Use: Pages 9 and 16.

Topic Sentence 2: Beyond marriage, women are shown to be sexual objects for men to enjoy.

Use: Pages 20, 21 and 26.

Topic Sentence 3: However, many women are just as ruthless and poorly behaved as men seem to be.

Use: Pages 15 and 19.

Topic Sentence 4: We are reminded that we are all equal, men and women alike.

Use: Pages 13 and 27.

How does the character of Mr Birling develop throughout the play?

Topic Sentence 1: Birling is the epitome of the arrogant, selfish upper class.

Use: Pages 10 and 22.

Topic Sentence 2: As the play goes on, we see his desperate need for authority and respect.

Use: Pages 8 and 9.

Topic Sentence 3: However, as the play develops he seems more and more foolish and ignorant.

Use: Pages 11, 28 and 29.

Topic Sentence 4: Essentially, Birling does not develop at all – he learns nothing and ends the play as ignorant as he began.

Use: Pages 30 and 31.

How is Eva Smith depicted in *An Inspector Calls*?

Topic Sentence 1: The beginning of Eva's troubles stem from the fact she is nothing more than a worker – she has very few rights.

Use: Pages 13 and 23.

Topic Sentence 2: However, she has many qualities which unfortunately lead to jealousy in others.

Use: Pages 14 and 15.

Topic Sentence 3: Furthermore, at times Eva is little more than a sexual object for men to attack.

Use: Pages 20, 21 and 24.

Topic Sentence 4: Fundamentally, she is representative of the entire working class.

Use: Pages 17, 19 and 27.

Suggested Revision Activities

Major character and themes – **Take any of the major characters and themes (see page 32 for a list) and group together quotations in sets of 2 or 3 to answer the following question: "How does the theme/character develop as the play goes on?"**

You should try to get 4 sets of quotations, giving you 8-12 overall.

A great cover and repeat exercise – **Cover the whole page, apart from the quotation at the top. Can you now fill in the four sections in your exercise book without looking – Interpretations, Techniques, Analysis, Use in essays on…?**

This also works really well as a revision activity with a friend **– cover the whole card, apart from the quotation at the top. If you read out the quotation, can they tell you the four sections without looking – Interpretations, Techniques, Analysis, Use in essays on…?**

"The Development Game" – **Pick any quotation at random from The Quotation Bank and use it to create an essay question, and then create a focused topic sentence to start the essay. Next, find another appropriate quotation to develop your idea even further.**

"The Contrast Game" – **Follow the same rules as The Development Game, but instead of finding a quotation to support your idea, find a quotation that can be used to start a counter-argument.**

Your very own Quotation Bank! **Using the same headings and format as The Quotation Bank, find 10 more quotations from throughout the text (select them from many different sections of the text to help develop whole text knowledge) and create your own revision cards.**

Essay writing – **They aren't always fun, but writing essays is great revision. Choose a practice question and then try taking three quotations and writing out a perfect paragraph, making sure you add connectives, technical vocabulary and sophisticated language.**

Glossary

Alliteration – Repetition of the same consonant or sound at the beginning of a number of words in a sentence: "hard-headed" has a cold tone, mimicking Birling's coldness towards his workers.

Dramatic Irony – When the audience knows something the characters don't: the Inspector has authority in his final speech as we know what he is saying comes true.

Euphemism – An indirect way of expressing something unpleasant: when Eric threatens to "make a row" he actually means he could get violent.

Imagery – Figurative language that appeals to the senses of the audience: "obscene fat carcass" makes Meggarty seem more like an animal than a person.

Irony – A statement that suggests one thing but often has a contrary meaning: Gerald says that young women should be protected, yet they all abuse Eva.

Juxtaposition – Two ideas, images or words placed next to each other to create a contrasting effect: "chap" seems entirely pleasant, yet "nasty" suggests the opposite.

Language – The vocabulary chosen to create effect.

Polysyndeton – The repetition of conjunctions such as "and" one after another: the "and" in "millions and millions and millions" increases the scale of the issue.

Repetition – When a word, phrase or idea is repeated to reinforce it: Sheila's constant repetition of "I" emphasises how selfish she is.

Rhetorical Questions – A persuasive device where the person asking the question already knows the answer: when the Inspector asks about protecting women, he knows the answer will trap Gerald.

Semantic Field – A group of words used together from the same topic area: "Lord Mayor", "Knighthood" and "Party" all show Birling's obsession with political power.

Sentence Structure – The way the writer has ordered the words in a sentence to create a certain effect: when talking to Gerald about Lady Croft's objections to Sheila, the stress falls on "socially".

Simile – A comparison of one thing with something of a different kind, used to make a description more vivid: "bees" depicts a group as entirely equal and working together.

Stage Directions – Directions given to the director or actor to aid interpretation: the lighting instructions at the beginning of the play give a visual representation of the play's key theme.

Symbolism – The use of a symbol to represent an idea: the bright light upon the arrival of the Inspector is symbolic of him shining a light on the Birling's behaviour.

Tri-colon – A list of three words or phrases for effect: "fire and blood and anguish" illustrate the full extent of human suffering if we don't learn the lessons of the play.